The Scientific Evidence of Dr Wang

The Scientific Evidence of Dr Wang

Stephanie de Montalk

VUP

VICTORIA UNIVERSITY PRESS
Victoria University of Wellington
PO Box 600, Wellington

ISBN 0 86473 441 7

First published 2002

Published with the assistance of a grant from

Printed by PrintLink, Wellington

FOR DAVID

CONTENTS

I

II

III

Acknowledgments

My grateful thanks to my husband, John Miller, for everything, as always.

I am also very grateful to Fergus Barrowman, Bill Manhire and James Brown for invaluable advice regarding selection of the poems, Brendan O'Brien for his wonderful artwork and cover design, Betty Wilson who prompted the writing of 'Notion', and Marg Tait who alerted me to the possibilities of offal, as recorded in 'Fifth Quarter'.

Further thanks are due to the editors of the following publications in which some of these poems, or earlier versions of them, first appeared: *Eleven Books from the Rita Angus Cottage* (printed and published by Brendan O'Brien), *JAAM*, *Spectacular Babies* (ed. Bill Manhire and Karen Anderson), *Sport*, *Southerly* (Australia), *London Magazine*, *Poetry NZ*, *Turbine*.

'Letter', 'Code of Practice', 'The Intransigent Traveller' and 'Style and Completeness' were written for my children, Jonathon, Melissa, Donovan and Dylan.

'Northern Spring' recalls British Minister of Labour and National Service, Ernest Bevin, who in 1940 forbade workers to leave or change their jobs without government permission.

'Style and Completeness', 'The King Who Did Not Want to Die' and 'Tree Marriage' take liberties with Athenian poet and statesman Solon (594), ancient Mesopotamian hero Gilgamesh, and Mrs Pobjoy, the last mistress of Beau Nash (who died 1761), respectively.

The opening lines of 'Felicity' adapt R.A.K. Mason's 'I often think of you as I roam by some secluded and delightful solitude', as written to Geoffrey Potocki de Montalk in January 1930; and 'The Retired Barrister' appropriates Louis Simpson's 'a picture drifted into my mind', from 'In Otto's Basement'.

I

A Compact Hand

The art of penmanship—
the whole art, that is,
of legibility—is economically
important. An act of trust.
An opening scene. The closest
thing we have to living speech.
An utterance, to put it bluntly,
of instrument and ink.

We must learn, therefore,
to develop good habits,
to be our own good teachers,
to put our tongues firmly
between our cheeks and teeth
and turn our untidy and sprawling
voices to their most pecuniary
advantage. The struggle may be
long, the relapses frequent, but
with rigour, slant and sleight
of line, sophistry should follow.

The Retired Barrister

He was dining out one night
when the conversation turned
to colonisation, justice and
trial by jury—
a subject he knew something about,
a system on which he had spent
valuable time when he could
have been reading Tolstoy,
Dickens and *The Decline and Fall
of the Roman Empire,*
or taking time out in unexpected
corners of the world like . . . Vladivostok,

and scenes drifted into his mind
from court rooms in Hong Kong
of juries which hadn't listened
to him, hadn't understood him,
had started off with the view
that the defendant was guilty
anyway, or they wouldn't be there,
and were simply waiting for the judge
to give them the answer.

He swallowed his wine
and tasted futility.
'It doesn't work!' he declared.
'It's a complete waste of time!
It's the sort of seemingly
sensible process
that brought about the mutiny,
the opium wars
and fifty-five days at Peking,
and I ask myself now
was it worth it—
searching for the right phrase,
the piece of Shakespeare,
staying up until three in the morning?

I would say,
"Members of the jury,
you may think the evidence
against my client
is overwhelming:
the fingerprints at the scene,
the confession at the police station,
the result of the identification parade,
the scientific evidence of Dr Wang;
but look at my client—
he is wearing a suit.
Would a man
who is wearing a suit
commit such a crime?"

And they would face me,
arms folded,
staring stonily ahead,
ignoring my arguments,
rejecting my pleas,

and the judge, who was writing,
would stop,
peer at me
and say impatiently,
"Get on with it, Mr Griffiths."'

Code of Practice

Mr Puji, brother of the last emperor,
engaged in light industry—bicycles,
fans and a rectangular article which could be
a cabin bag or toaster—also produces

more traditional products. For example,
in accordance with the Ming Dynasty
and energetic networks between
fingers, gall bladder and spleen,

he manufactures exercise balls
of high quality for the hand. Impressing
with his independence, he sculpts
the once wooden form hollow,

lacquers the surface and, with the sun
over the heron sanctuary, ice on the
imperial bridge and his rainbow
collection of goldfish returned to its tub

after spawning, installs a vibrating plate
for increased effectiveness. While he
does not promise regular use of his
iron device will improve the soundness

of body and mind, he maintains that
quivering bars in multiples of nine
may be used to auspicious effect
and his factory, which conforms to the

shape of the universe and features
a fifteenth-century bell,
has a certificate of good health,
stamped 1985 to prove it.

...ise

the end of the day,
...nkful for the river
...ich scatters the gold leaves
stretches and pounds

the green light he beats
...tween paper and skin

...d later, the thin sheets
...e places on leather
...r the delicate act of cutting,

...e artisan acknowledges his small role
...n the tableaux of trinkets,
...dging and illumination
...f manuscripts,

...he history of masterpieces
...rought to perfection

only to be melted
and mixed easily with water

or upturned beneath
sumptuous and biblical skies,

and his dependence on men
who, having tapped rich veins,
now breathe slowly
in rectangular rooms.

He understands that his floor
will recall neither pedestals
nor outstretched hands,

that his anvil has no memory
of clamour.

Exercise Master

You wake to the bounce
of first light
from building to building,

from hot, heavily gated
window and door

to the clearance sale
fifty percent below
import price
permanently, from China,

your mission the safe
delivery of passengers
travelling from, say
Auckland or Melbourne,

to American breakfasts
in stopover hotels

and pavements on which
they can stroll
and think about teapots,
pewter and soccer-ball clocks
to take home

and the imprecise outline
of your city with its original
shops, courthouses
and prisons,

to the long continuation
of their journey
on which say, above
the Bay of Bengal,

baton in hand,
three thousand, four hundred
and thirty two miles from Mecca
in a northwesterly direction,

you will again demonstrate
the art of pumping the knees,
circling the ankles,
marching
and breathing normally,

your seat upright,
your face cool,
the sky sailing, rolling gently.

Famou

Conside

the one
from friv

and walk
easy snow
rain whisp
in the dist

See him liv

turning thii
to the busin
of self-mort
and subsiste

searching fo

opposing ext
in public wor
and over-cohe
in architectur
and banking.

Perhaps he is t
scarecrows
and leaden dar

and the rise
and methodical
of breathing?

Po

At
th
wl
he

to
be

a
h
f

t
i
e

t

Serrations

A tall breeze scatters apples,
herbs and the small signs
still propped against stalls,

and the solderer,
who works in a franking machine factory
and thinks about postal museums
and his own table
at an international exhibition in Berlin
displaying the stamps he designs
in the evening
at his desk
with its incandescent lamp
and reliable assortment
of brushes and inks,

adjusts his protective glasses
and reduces the next
unwieldy sheet of steel
to a perfect square.

Within a month the markets
will have fastened their awnings,
cognac and cheese will no longer
be available to tourists
and the breeze
which blows down
from the underbrush,
gritty and careless of memory
and the ever-present
snow of the sky,
will drop sycamore wings
and other chance seedlings
on rocks, ferries
and the dark glass of the sea.

The solderer kicks
the dust at his feet,
the cool air at the door.
Soon he will need
to clean out his cellar,
tie back his gate
and place his melons and outdoor
chairs in safe keeping.
He serrates the freshly shaved
metal and thinks about
a range of seals for Christmas—
something more topical
than sleighs and strategically
placed shadows,
less certain
than antlers and bells—
but the options seem limited:
wildlife offers so few
stylistic opportunities,
vegetation is hardly appropriate
and, while patriotic symbolism is popular,
daggers, belted tunics
and the windowless towers
in which animals once sheltered
and prayers were said
would only cause confusion.

He smooths the outer side
of the panel to a dull gleam
and scores it with a number.
The arched dam in the mountains
is nearing completion,
eagerly awaited by monasteries,
sanatoria and institutions
which know about winter,
and might be a means
of resolving the problem;
also the proposed block

Exercise Master

You wake to the bounce
of first light
from building to building,

from hot, heavily gated
window and door

to the clearance sale
fifty percent below
import price
permanently, from China,

your mission the safe
delivery of passengers
travelling from, say
Auckland or Melbourne,

to American breakfasts
in stopover hotels

and pavements on which
they can stroll
and think about teapots,
pewter and soccer-ball clocks
to take home

and the imprecise outline
of your city with its original
shops, courthouses
and prisons,

to the long continuation
of their journey
on which say, above
the Bay of Bengal,

baton in hand,
three thousand, four hundred
and thirty two miles from Mecca
in a northwesterly direction,

you will again demonstrate
the art of pumping the knees,
circling the ankles,
marching
and breathing normally,

your seat upright,
your face cool,
the sky sailing, rolling gently.

Famous Blue Raincoat

Consider the dissident—

the one who abstains
from frivolous small talk

and walks in the mountains
easy snow on his back and bare feet,
rain whispering
in the distance.

See him living in caves,

turning thin obedient wrists
to the business
of self-mortification
and subsistence farming,

searching for impermanence,

opposing extravagance
in public works
and over-coherent systems
in architecture
and banking.

Perhaps he is bringing back
scarecrows
and leaden darkness

and the rise
and methodical fall
of breathing?

Poise

At the end of the day,
thankful for the river
which scatters the gold leaves
he stretches and pounds

to the green light he beats
between paper and skin

and later, the thin sheets
he places on leather
for the delicate act of cutting,

the artisan acknowledges his small role
in the tableaux of trinkets,
edging and illumination
of manuscripts,

the history of masterpieces
brought to perfection

only to be melted
and mixed easily with water

or upturned beneath
sumptuous and biblical skies,

and his dependence on men
who, having tapped rich veins,
now breathe slowly
in rectangular rooms.

He understands that his floor
will recall neither pedestals
nor outstretched hands,

that his anvil has no memory
of clamour.

of high density housing,
an impression of which
could be sketched
from the plaster replica
at the town hall.

The breeze snatches what it can
from the street: fate, intoxication,
the skirts of priests and beautiful women.
Steel filings shift on the floor.

The solderer fetches a broom.
The energy of the arched dam?
The heat of a compact apartment?

He feeds his time sheet into a meter.
Floodwaters, spillways, daylight, a microwave—
he might even
go as far as a catalogue.

Violinist at the Edge of an Ice Field

At first only silence,

and then slowly a dull roar
as if sediment is rising
from past climates
and ridges of soil
are shifting the bedrock,

and the scrape of horsehair
on resin, or a string which has yet
to be tightened
and could be grains of ice
squeezing the air,

a crevasse stretching,

or a solidified stream adjusting
to shear stress
and the immediate prospect
of decoupling,

and she knows she will need
to loosen herself up,

take herself down
to the level of science,

dismiss the mythical beast
beneath the surface
and try to believe
the glacier is little more
than hexagonal plates, needles
and stars which have lost
their sharp edge
and developed an interesting
crystalline structure,

that the atomic
arrangement of ice is boring
and best described as
a system of circles

and that, according to quantum theory,
this moment, this second,
this aged and uncertain
stretch of the planet

is only the tip of an iceberg
and computers
can handle anything.

In danger now of travelling too far
she places the laws of physics on hold,

tells herself
that in times of extremity
recollection of pleasure
can be useful

and thinks about her garden—
her sprinkler teasing the lawn,

the wide hips of her roses
swaying across fences,

her daphne growing wild
and covered with cobwebs—

and Stravinsky—the opera,
the concert, the silent
explosion . . .

no! she cancels Stravinsky
and returns to the cobwebs.

Here, she assumes the weighted
excellence of a spider,

imagines she has segmented
legs which will grow again
if she breaks them,

produces silk,

slides herself onto the ice,
her body tiny and slender,
her tongue lined with teeth,

applies her crampons and axe
to the surface
and starts picking her way
across the river—

sharp, connected and deadly.

Showers in the River Basin

CNN predicts teachers
tapping their desks
in silent classrooms,

reflecting that although
they have additional
responsibilities as health
workers and managers
of domestic airports,
life passes quietly enough

and tonight they will drive
home satisfied that, malaria,
yellow fever and sleeping
sickness aside, they
quarrelled with no one today,
nor will they

given their solitary verandahs
and bedrooms shaded by rain,

the confused merging
and branching of kittens
and songbirds
left behind by their wives

who decided that cribbage
could no longer be scored
with pencil and paper

and Saturday cricket
in the debris of river banks
would only result in
dismissal without runs;

given their stand against respiratory
illness and intestinal parasites;

their preoccupation with light
satire and imitations of nonsense

and their quarterly publications
about food safety and airline security—
subjects they'll reinvent in novels
to be written in retirement.

*

CNN also predicts
needlework,

the fatigued singing
of frogs,

smoke passing through
low
evening skies.

Without Tune

East of Alaska,
before Siberia,

winter closing
on bare committed air,

encampments thick
with driftwood, turf

and piling snow,
the shore pushing itself

as far south
as it can manage

from the lost sounds
of the tundra

*

they spread their feet
on soft ground.

*

The land, sky and what was left
of the sea

came splendidly together,
pensive moments

of colour
receded without tune,

the world was a plateau,
newly serene and spectacular.

*

'We had to come,' they said.
'There were campaigns

for the fingerprinting
of infants,

construction firms were urging
the purchase of safety film

for windows and French doors
and keepers were being attacked

by wild animals in zoos
on national television.'

*

No one responded.
Only scraps

of their conversation
were heard,

only parts of their language
remained.

*

They assimilated swiftly,
without speaking.

Some played the meagre harp,
some the one-sided drum,

others danced
as the occasion dictated.

Time moved
intermittently.

Light passed
without problems.

*

They occupied themselves
with practical divisions of labour:

tethering reindeer,
raising children,

sewing small skins
with precision;

accepted apprenticeships
in whatever came naturally:

the soul of animal,
the lamp of stone,

the ritual
song of magic;

watched clans became tribes,
tribes become clans,

fixed routes dissolve
into lichen.

*

The willows returned,
the sea returned,

cliffs, rocks and
shadows returned

*

and all flourished
briefly

as custom demanded.

Sea Monkey

You're at sea

in fine lines of grass
and the logical flow
of the current

attempting to reach
the ocean

on the only ship left
in the navy.

*

History has not yet recorded
your necessary
and tumultuous events—

you are too new,
too uninterrupted,

still too easily startled
and unwilling to blend
with the rocky floor
or coral outcrop,

still aware that
your predecessor, who
submitted without hesitation
and sank thankfully
in shallow water,

now rests in an algae-
covered shelter.

*

The weather turns.

*

You adjust engine, ballast
and ropes in accordance
with your training,

your back upright
against the shoreline,

trousers, jacket and cap
slanting only slightly

as waves open
in mid air
above the deck,

a hundred carefully assembled
parts shudder

and a discerning wind
eschewing pine trees
and grassy banks

calls for broadcast quality
images of your descent

*

to be followed by masks,
puppetry
and juggling equipment

via sonar
and remote feedback—

evidence
of the way you once lived.

Tree Marriage

When the dandy of Bath died
his mistress put dust

covers over his tailor
and wigmaker and left

his Palladian mansion
to live in a tree

surrounded by heartwood,
broad leaves and, no longer

in need of clothing,
admiration in a natural setting.

She bought an embroidery frame
on which to record her impressions

of silence, shade and the beat
of rain in the branches,

themes of soil and sky,
observations only possible

some distance from the ground,
abstractions she could work up

into tapestries
at a later stage.

*

The tree's girth was her temple
its limbs her romantic imagination—

all olive brown in the evening
and at dawn as pale and grey as King Arthur.

*

She also recovered her sense of theatre
and original freshness,

learnt to be patient
with lichen and rough skin

and careful with candles
and winter fires

which she lit
in small tins.

Style and Completeness

The lawmaker has posted
his reforms and reinforced
them with public recitations
of his poetry.

Slaves will be freed,
wealth will be measured
in wine, grain and equal
harvests of the soil

and trade in pottery
and olive oil will be increased.

Poverty will end in Attica!

*

Of course, there are complaints.

His treatment of political issues
is too lengthy,
his vocabulary is too plain,
his view of life too moderate
and optimistic.

'Where are grief and loss?'
he is asked.
'The outer limits?
The worst possibilities?

The gulf between Olympus
and suffering man?'

*

The lawmaker is displeased.

He has spent the summer
balancing and refining
his constitution,
abolishing serfdom
and freeing 'those who . . .
trembled at their masters' whims'.

'Why,' he might have written
'must I adjust my Athenian tongue?'

*

Nonetheless, he tugs at his chiton.

*

The next day he visits his mother
who welcomes him with
an inventory of the items
she will be taking
to the other side:
scarves, brooches, ribbons,
a hundred pairs of sandals
and soft shoes,
a hundred tunics in wool
and thin linen.

*

The lawmaker looks east and west
and attends to his beard.

*

'No one should go down
with more than three
sets of clothing,' he says.

'But life is hot, and boring,'
she reminds him.
'Levitation's impossible,
there's no future in geology,

no change from the coin
we will place in our mouths
for the river man
and little chance the many-
headed dog will be persuaded
to fetch and carry.'

'Then we should all be buried
with board games,' he replies

*

and hurries home to

write another elegy,

post another decree
in the marketplace,

apply himself to message,
metre and couplets
with his customary discretion

and in several striking tongues.

Northern Spring

A thousand steps
beneath cathedral

and clean sun,
beyond the brush

of hazel and pine,
the Bevin boys

born in Station Street
a mile from the tracks

above the shop of a baker
who made the best pies

ever tasted
wonder whether they should

mow their green heaths
now that the daffodils

are starting to fade,
now that the buttercup

fields of rape seed
are knee high.

*

One laments the loss
of his motorbike

and RAF uniform
during the war;

the other his brief career
as a shepherd,

his border collie—
some say the best dog

for the job—
and small knowledge

of animal behaviour,
although it goes

without saying
that a sheep can remember

a fair life
and more than fifty human faces.

*

New leaves
over shale and soft water,

new winds
on the weather report.

*

Aspirin
to thin the blood.

Sotolol
to slow the heart.

On the Dresser:

candlesticks,
a decanter,
six goblets,

*

the burnished
whinnying
of horses

*

and the strange
apricot chanting
of psalms.

Arrival

'Is the house
warm

in winter?'
they say,

'the walls
are so thin

there is sky
at the tips

of our fingers.
Will the chill

surround us?
the heat

scorch us?
the wind,

trees
and crackle-brown

lawns remain
at a distance?

We are not
accustomed

to the nearness
of seasons.

At home
they move

slowly
through stone.'

A Digression

1

Halfway between Caloundra and Noosa,
Mum, Dad and a couple of kids
came to The Place of Nets—
plenty of sand and surf,
but very little shade.

A pirate and sailor in hot velvet
were re-enacting the boarding of a boat
on the wharf

and Dad was asked to step forward
and ram a wad of wool
into the short barrel of a musket
and ignite a small cannon.

Mum watched with her fingers
in her ears, and the kids ate hamburgers,
every bit as interested.

2

The next day, Dad bought a gaily
scored shirt from a convenience store

and Mum a second-hand book
about the life and opinions
of an eighteenth-century gentleman,

while the kids played beneath
the useful eye of a life-guard
and signs outlining emergency procedures
in four languages.

That evening, there was a barbecue
in the condominium car park

after which Dad stayed on
for a few beers

and Mum returned to the apartment
with the kids
in time for 'The People's Vet'.
She was halfway through her book,
but although the midwife
had been mentioned,
the hero had yet to be born.

3

Sunrise at four-thirty,
on the beach before seven,
at six the sudden onset
of the full-bodied moon

and, in between, hot dogs,
coffee, an occasional copy
of *The Australian*,
the passing of a politician

and a primate at an easel
demonstrating its talent
for aesthetic order and balance.
'I'd like to let it loose on
your shirt and my book,' said Mum.

4

When the kids became bored
they went to the mall
and played video games,

and the ice-cream parlour
where scooping took place
behind the whiteness of counters.

Now and then they lay
beneath purposeful shade
while Mum talked about Uncle Toby
who'd been hit in the groin
with a stone
and Dr Sop who had fallen
from his horse

and delivery by forceps:
her hero had been born
and his nose broken
in the process.

5

The week wore on.

The sun was a steady white fire.
More and more families arrived
to start barbecues and experience
the persistent music of crows.
Bush sticks slammed against spiders
and Dad kept a look out for magpies.

The formerly discreet population
became shapeless as it presented itself
to the light, all things apparent,

as mould hardened on the world's
largest ginger factory,

as vintners were unable to offer
dessert wines owing to the honeyed
absence of *botrytis cinerea*
and kids caught their toes on the coral.

Mum's book was by now going nowhere.
'Rain might make a nice change,' she remarked.
'The sky's too tight across the desert,' said Dad.

Bar and Grill

Winter. Rain. Lamplight.

The sort of evening on which
assertions might be made
about the history of the universe,

or the strange orbit of Cruithne
(near companion of the earth
and pronounced Croo-een-ya)

which has been to the forefront
of their thinking following an article
in the scientific magazine of a friend.

They take their seats and peer skywards
but are immediately disturbed from behind
by the crumbling and terrible trouble Hazel

is having with her spine,
and the cattery into which
her kitten will be placed

when she visits her sister in Sydney.
Hazel details the purchase of a new
transporter and collar and says,

'He's never been in one before
and here I am, putting him in one.'
They say, 'Yes, well, of course,

in the absence of the journal
we're guessing that its somewhat unusual orbit
was first announced in 1980,'

Fifth Quarter

We hum original scores,

settle ourselves
at an afternoon table

and plan our annual occasion effortlessly
as always
*

starting with a passionfruit
cocktail on the lawn, perhaps

with canopies, shakers and bells,

the rotary clothesline
dismantled,

the frontage pleasantly
clear of pine needles

and along the mixed border
reinforcing the romance
of deer fern and blue carpet,

an African thumb piano
and ripple of lavender.

Someone suggests a martini,
or a lager on account of the froth,

but put to the vote the analogy
of the passionfruit plant's
petals, stamen and filament
to the apostles and crown of thorns
so beloved of Jesuit missionaries in South America
is unanimously retained

leaving only the estimation
of pulp and seed in the pan
and the all-important selection
of pink flowers for their sprinkling
and sedative effect.

*

Tea and coffee are taken.

Connections between palate
and animated conversation are made, like

crab cakes to regulators,
wetsuits and a possible son away
on a diving course,

his bleached hair
floating and streaming,
his tubed air
clicking and hissing,
fish and fine sand
drifting and staring,

or pasta to carbon monoxide
and small white cars
bumper to bumper in Rome,

or pastry to the fastidious
kneading of dough,
and a daughter
about to marry again,

*

even chicken cooked under a brick—
two heated carefully balanced
foil-wrapped bricks, to be exact—
to greaseproof paper in home baking

and at a stretch, acacia trees
in the Sudanese desert where gum arabic
is extracted for use in food thickeners
and ink.

*

Easy discussion about fat, fear of which
has ruled out lamb, pork and canned tuna,

follows the absence of fibre
in cattle

and the fact that venison and veal,
once minced and masqueraded
as lentil loaf or exotic donkey
sausage, will no longer be acceptable

now that everyone is serving
crème brûlée for dessert.

*

The heating is increased.

Sherry is offered
and accepted

and Bobby Darin can be heard
singing 'Mack the Knife'
cautiously in the kitchen.

*

The rural member raises a hand
concerned that salads, satays and things herbal
will affect discussion of pipe replacement

and is advised that beekeeping once arose
from a starter which consisted almost entirely
of tomato,

and an urban representative
notes that snow peas should not be substituted
for cow peas, or yellow-eyed *gunga*—
otherwise known as pigeon peas—

even though neither is locally available.

*

Crackers are produced,

a platter of cheese,

a raffish casket of wine.

*

Those with families phone home
and excuse themselves from the evening meal

prompting comment about the role of women
in the perpetuation of junk food

*

and chance examination of a cookbook
featuring sea salt, red tea with silenium
and, hanging from a dark beam
in a hut in the Balkans,

strings of paprika in clear vibrant colour:

*

pages which make us eager to peel, purée and eat
at a rickety table,

store white beans in a bucket
and count them out on a bed,

pile pans on black earth
in a corner for the boiling of
kidney and liver with taro and yam.

*

We anticipate tripe in ladles of stock,

fritot of pancreas
and thymus gland

and gradually,
glossy, bedabbled and clean-shaven,

a windpipe and lung

varied to taste with capers,
bristling with rice and, thistlelike,

the greyish green buds
of the artichokes
we will grow in our adventurous gardens.

Café Dionysus

Each evening
we reach
for the weighted branch
of the vine,
steady
our expert gaze,
taste,
name
and pour,
cork moist,
temperature just so,

recalling
immortal connections,
contributions
to courage and wisdom
and the lyrical inspiration
with which history
was once placed
on water carriers
and walls.

Our tongues rediscover
their magic,
our delicacy
its flash of genius,
and each night
we remain
at our posts,
patiently absorbing
enrichment
and simultaneous
acts of kindness.

Contrast Medium

You arrive at Reception,
having glimpsed the room
in which your intravenous
procedure will be performed

through a momentary gap
in the door—

the room, that is, in which
prone in your seamless
cotton garment,

dentures and hairpins removed,
green vegetables and aerated
drinks omitted for 48 hours,
water and medicines
for the previous twelve,

a radio-opaque dye
will light up your head,
kidneys, heart
and, like the Blackpool illuminations,
the various connections between—

and can't remember
the name of the specialist
who referred you.

You say to the receptionist,
'I think it begins with F,'
and 'the surgery is somewhere
between the beach
and botanical gardens . . .

it doesn't appear to be
in the phonebook . . .'

but she is speaking to Fatima
who has forgotten
her appointment
and will probably have to wait
until February for another one.

*

In the day room
a man in jeans
adjusts his sneakers
and reads 'At Home with the Arctic Wolf'
in *National Geographic*—

specifically the fold-out page
on which three wolves
stalk seven musk oxen
standing in a semicircle
on cotton grass

backlit and blinded by silver—

and Mr Graham is asked to
'Take a call on line zero.
A call on line zero.'

You examine a wall-sized silhouette
of the Sydney Harbour Bridge

at daybreak
or nightfall

and a display case
of bright tissue and bone:

the ribbed interiors
of female tuataras
numbers one and seven,
enhanced for purposes
of egg detection

and the rangy pelvis of Jambi
the twelve-year-old tiger
who had a 'sore and stiff back'
because he no longer entertained
folklore, or moonlit nights
in ruined temples and courts—

light seeping through shadow,
motifs of bark, rock and cave—

and seat yourself.

*

A technician walks by
with a clipboard and straight
hair—tidy indications
of competence

should anaphylaxis occur

and adrenalin, intubation
and artificial respiration
be required.

*

The coloured fish pulsate
in their cylinder

outwardly calm,
swimming well,

manoeuvring themselves
in hopeful directions.

Solatium (1)

In your room
another visitor

leaving,
and you

in the memory
of stillness.
*

Are our smiles
too bright?

Is our talk
too small:

the meals,
the match

against the Aussies,
Jonah

on the bench,
your prediction—

the All Blacks
by twelve—

and today
the flowering of alpine tussock

foretelling
a long summer?
*

They say
you've asked

for extreme unction,
used words like

chivalry and gallantry
hardly heard any more.

It seems
the term is healing.

Solatium (2)

You might have been
humming

in a forest filled
with orchids

and other
tropical flowers

the way you were
standing there

close
to the ceiling.

We opened the door,
offered

soft bread,
hoped you'd come down,

fold your wings,
slip away

into the finely
tuned night.

Night Note

You will leave
early,
before the thin

clink
of thermometers
and well-wishers,

before the washing
and brushing
and rattling

of the trolley
in the adjoining
room, before

the report
can be written.
You will breathe

above the sea,
float
like a shellfish

which has freed
itself
from an undated

cave, unaware
that the charts
have been

gathered in,
that the tea
which has been

poured
and left
on your locker

is still as warm
as the red
morning

is brief
but believable.

Tremor

Today,
trees
leaning into the wind.

*

Tonight,
only twenty minutes
of uninterrupted sleep.

*

Tomorrow,
a strenuous piano,

and water,
fresh fruit
and the act of swallowing

less readily available.

*

Will access to the slender bird
on its bright orange
background cease?

the biographies be recalled?

the seven small stones
returned to the earth

and the leather gloves
and twopenny broadsheet
released, for ever,

mildew no match
for sincerity?

What will become
of the radish garden

and perforated lace
borders of the eggcups
and plates of the Royal
Copenhagen collection
in the china cabinet?

The fisheye lens
which enhanced each
of the five satellites of Uranus
with the translucent form
of a grasshopper

and realigned the membership
of the photographic society

(although it was later said
that the stand taken
on the sprinkler system
in the darkroom
was also responsible)?

*

The next day,
loss of the strength
and lustre of carefully
cut hair,

*

and the day after that,
the pilgrimage to India—

Shiva
pressing the mountain down
with his toe.

Last Settlement

She enters the imperial villa,
world of the once beautiful.
A clear broth is placed before her,
a meat dish, easily managed
with a spoon
and an advantageous dessert.
The wind and sea
cannot touch her,
the bronzed doors
will not open,
the vestibule is lonely
and she knows
that the oils she once poured
and the attractive hours
she once scattered
are finally without significance.
Mirrors wait in the distance,
roses and torpid water
assume importance.
She loses her way in carpeted
corridors, detours to the teas
and thoughtfully placed
cakes in the kitchenettes
of the visitors,
sings the half-remembered
song of the sun and the rain
and hopes for a shape,
a column,
a deeply lobed leaf,
an acanthus plant
in the forest of walls.
Her physical details
are not remembered,
her virtues are unlisted,
and the importance of gesture
and artistic order

in the biographical scene
which will feature
on her sarcophagus
has been settled without her.

She has entered the imperial villa,
home of the once beautiful.
Her greatness will be decided for her.

Letter

Last weekend the wind
brought cobalt skies,
bright hills and cicadas
louder than you're likely
to remember them.
The cats slept in new grass,
leaves swirled
on the lower lawn,
and all day there was a deep
white light, and everything
with an edge to it.

Depth of Field

They speak of Italian
and Afghan skies
as they travel
to the ends
of the earth
in search of dunes
and salted monuments
to admire
from every
conceivable angle.
They eat rice
from lightly
fired bowls,
drink soups
of unknown
origin,
and fresh
with all that is
knowing
and new
accept everything
pressed upon them,
agile
in front of a star-
spangled bus
and their own
roving camera.

Hotel Hungary

The package included airfares,
transfers, views of rivers
and resisting horses

and of course a hotel
with a kiosk selling stamps
and bottled water

and a bed in which they could
dream the deep dreams of the day
before descending to a friendly

and substantial breakfast.
But on arrival, while the statues
and marble lobby were to their liking

there were cracks in the foreign currency counter
and they were disappointed
with the puckered carpet in the corridor

and the vastness of the dining room
in which a traveller was sitting alone,
languishing as if in a private collection

of candelabras and table napkins
and the shadows of too many waiters,
bending over his dumplings

as a manservant might after hours
over a soup and solitary potato,
or a party after the necessary

romps and interventions,
the takings of umbrage ever-so-slightly,
the traditional handling of gloves

and later the discovery
of a guest in a side room,
eating crackers and paste alongside

the rugs, books and decanters,
the paintings and pale walls,
the cleared desk,

with the door half ajar,
the hall barely lit,
and the appetite and laughter between.

Felicity

I often think of you as I roam by
secluded and delightful solitudes:

buffalo, deer, wild boar,
rivers assuming the colours

of grasslands and trees
and lakes the evening patience

of watering holes.
I think of you in vineyards,

citrus orchards and caves misty
with waterfalls—or cataracts

as your father used to call them—
and wonder whether I should attempt

a sonnet, or a scholarly translation
or the all-important sighing,

tapering and waning of the libretto
we once started . . .

ah the libretto—its companionless
tributaries, verbal mannerisms

and final white spaces of sky;
its lonely rolling moon

and sun, far from the hasty design
and centre of things

and us, infrequent figures in fantasy,
less concerned with what we were doing

than the way we were doing it,
immersed in refrains of victory and defeat

in which greatness was touched by vengeance
and women and children by immortality.

I think of you also in deserted cemeteries,
cinemas and gymnasiums,

in the creak of libraries
and religious festivals,

in the unlikely
        glitter of riddles,

the unmistakable
        grace of geese.

SPQR

In the morning
the Cardinals' Palace Gardens,

at dusk, dinner
on the loggia
overlooking the city
and the labyrinthine route
by which they returned
in the late afternoon
to the concrete cool
of their rooms
and thin white beds.

*

The wind lifted early summer dust
from the street,
whiter than vapour,
lighter than an original dream,
a swirl of champagne
between bottle and glass
in the glittering hour
before sunset.
Fashion houses and hotels
sparkled with promise,
the Trevi Fountain was heavy
with treasure and the clatter
of publicly loved children
and expensive small talk
could be heard beneath the Plane Trees
in the Via Vittorio Veneta.
Mature flowers shed petals with abandon.
Words came slowly,
small phrases at a time.

An acquaintance living locally,
spoke of noise levels,
motor vehicle control
and the placement of schools,
indistinguishable from his wife
in cream cotton trousers;
the traffic howled;
olive trees hid in the darkness
of small lights, while
behind the Caelian Hill,
on the river flats,
corridors of shrewdly lit marble
glowed in the windows
of the Ministry of Posts
and Telecommunications
where employees working late
ate grapes and figs
with their fingers
and drank jugs of soft water
and wine.

Wolves appeared on the threshold.
Statues rose out of the walls.
Gladiators fell through the frescoes—
they might have been ivory.

Dog on a Mountain

With no direct route to the sea
we were lost, totally lost,
driving up and down mountains,
eyeing snow caps and rocky brown tussock
and hoping the coast
and warm order of room
would be ours before nightfall.

The roads were unsealed
and there was very little traffic,
only an occasional trader
carrying gas canisters and plastic,
strolling as if from the city
to disconnected settlements
between foothills.

The menace of absence
and exile of Ovid came to mind—
black winters, black seas,
a muddy outpost;
barbarians coming down from the hills;
gods, Latin, transformation
and statues celebrating
conspicuous emotion
a full autumn and summer away—
and we wished we'd packed matches
and a pot to make tea
for there were streams
and plenty of sticks around.

A dog appeared on a ridge behind us
and howled, and howled
from the back of its throat,
affronted perhaps by a squall in the valley
or a scarcity of field mushrooms,
its voice heavy,

its song cold,
its heart locked in unwanted earth.

We spoke briefly of Tomis
at the edge of the Empire,
and Marchesi who taught Melba
to sing through her nose,
thereby preserving her vocal cords,

and pressed on,
positioning the compass
and reviewing the map with increased interest,

the animal less lonely over distance,
less troubled,
less intensely connected.

Notion

Tout est pour le mieux dans le meilleur
des mondes possibles.
—Voltaire

There was the bleakness
of the oilskin coat
which dripped furiously
over her feet

and the concierge who agreed
in excellent English
that the week had been

'miserable,
very depressing,
yes, really very, very depressing'.

*

There was the advertisement in *Time Out*
asking for sculptors and artists
to repair an old mill,

the desire to gather oak
from old pews and carve it,

the girl who jumped from a window
in Earls Court,

the boy who had spent too long
on a kibbutz,

and the possibility of witchcraft.

*

And there was the wig she was wearing
because wigs were the fashion
in the Aeroflot queue
at the airport in Moscow

where a guard with a gun
looked at her passport and shouted

even though she was saying,
'You've a beautiful country
with spires and tanks and snow
in Red Square, and tall soldiers with hats . . .'

*

and the article that said
there was nothing in physics
that ruled out
future-or-past-directed
time travel.

The Intransigent Traveller

has gone to the farm
but doesn't think
he will stay
more than a couple
of days:
he has a situation with cattle
which can be seen
from dining room windows,
other people's plates
and India
north of Delhi
where a waiter
with three thumbs
once served him
an omelette.

Cha-Cha-Cha

I was once a helicopter pilot
commissioned to take aerial photographs
of a railroad extension

and produce images
as white and hard
as the moon.

*

Because my work was
highly regarded

I was given a room with a hand basin
and view of the heather

at the Junction Hotel.

*

Sweet heather!

I was soon caught in the gaze
of that sweet, blue heather.

*

By day I made what I could
of the parallel lines
and beds of roughly crushed stone

and in the evening I disappeared
in a cloud of wine, wearing my scarf

*

leaving an impression of
indigo
and wind-blown spray

and the tango
which was making a comeback.

The King Who Did Not Want to Die

Gilgamesh,
having fled the persistent
marriage proposals
of Ishtar, goddess of love,

and the divine bull
she sent to destroy him,

and all the other pressures
and trials of a Sumerian king—
widows, orphans, copious streams,
literate and troublesome
communities and navigational
bottlenecks at Baghdad—

is reclining in a distant forest
writing an epic poem
about his marble rule
of southern Mesopotamia

and making satisfactory progress
with date palms and reeds—cedar work
he will probably use as barter
for the sapling of youth
which, coincidentally, grows there
and, described as a child of the moon
with a pale and feathery appearance,
he is bound to recognise.

The remoteness of his situation
appeals enormously.
Weeks pass with only trees to confound him,
without the usual grim reports
of the netherworld; and each morning
he whistles as he greets the sun—
clad as if for a courtly encounter,

although once the ceremony,
which also includes chanting, is complete
he removes the robe and folds it
in existing creases.

However, there is still the matter
of the sapling to contend with
(so far the plant has not been forthcoming)

and at night, as he arranges himself
in his leaf-covered area,
on his bolster of skin and soft bracken,
lips drawn, breath set,
he engages in earnest discussion
about trickery . . . and uncertainty;

the possibility that his carvings
may not survive
and his epic tablets, which have a
realistic chance of exaltation,
at least in his lifetime,
will not be discovered complete.

Life to Defend

In the course
of his loyalty

he bent his ear
to the king's wish,

his hand
to the king's dish,

his net
to the king's fish—

royal sturgeon,
beluga,

valued
for its longevity,

and, given its
eagerness

to engage
in heated argument

with authorities
and scandal

with passing strangers,
prone

to entrapment
and at risk of fatigue.

Celebration

Recently, after rain,
we praised a butterfly
clinging
to a breezy day.
Now, ancient seeds

in caves suggest
we might once have planted
flowering stalks loosely
in dry earth,
firmly in the blue

bones of crevices
and mossy track marks
of subterranean streams,
arranged them
individually

and infallibly
according to fragrance,
shape and dancing
colour, and admired
them through morning

calm and the rest
of the day's bright carnival
until the hills passed
into their various
shades of darkness.

Stonework

As for solitude
should I

mention
the ferry

leaving
the clay house

suddenly
bereft

of summer
the lake

cradled
between forest

and mountain?
Should I remember

its unexpected clarity
after the wind

had thrown us
laughing

into the air
after steel

glass
and the high

angled wall
of the city?

In the Arboretum

endless
clear air,

the sun
easy

on north walls,
a tenure

of small chores.
*

Trees
with Venetian

red hair,
the optimism

of maples,
the late

skins of apples,
*

the freedoms
and limitations

of sparrows.

The Same Constellation

They sit at a window,
order jasmine tea

and wild rice
on lotus leaves

and try to recall
the dried lines of fish

along the pavement,
the pragmatic clutter

of survival
on the long, humid

edge of the harbour
and the neon brilliance

of the Temple of Heaven.
But the wild rice

remains pressed to the page,
stifling the scent

of its dampness,
withholding the heat

of its monsoon sky.

Notes Along the Cool Edge of a Page

August

You'll have summer at your window
now

and in your small square fields
thorny plants,

dry skies
and olive trees

in pairs—
loose white clusters,

lance-shaped leaves,
in bloom

since May,
since Homer.

December

The thin pale days
and early frosts

of the harvest
are here.

Each year the gathering
is less difficult.

You'll spread your blankets
tree by tree

beneath the green
and silver leaves,

shake the stems
and

let the olives fall—
anywhere

it does not matter
where.

April

Last night, soft rain
on the roof of the *cabanon,*

this morning
damp sun,

new flowers,
and the sky pulling back

from the urgent landscape
of spring.

Your trees may not bloom
this year,

they vary
season to season,

but their leaves
are certain,

their trunks
indestructible,

their oil clear gold
on glass.